Release Anger from

Shitty People

The Vulgar and Delightful Adult Coloring Book

By

S.B. Nozaz

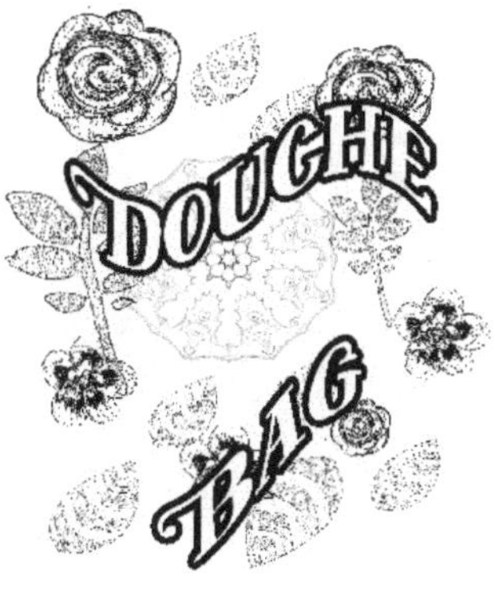

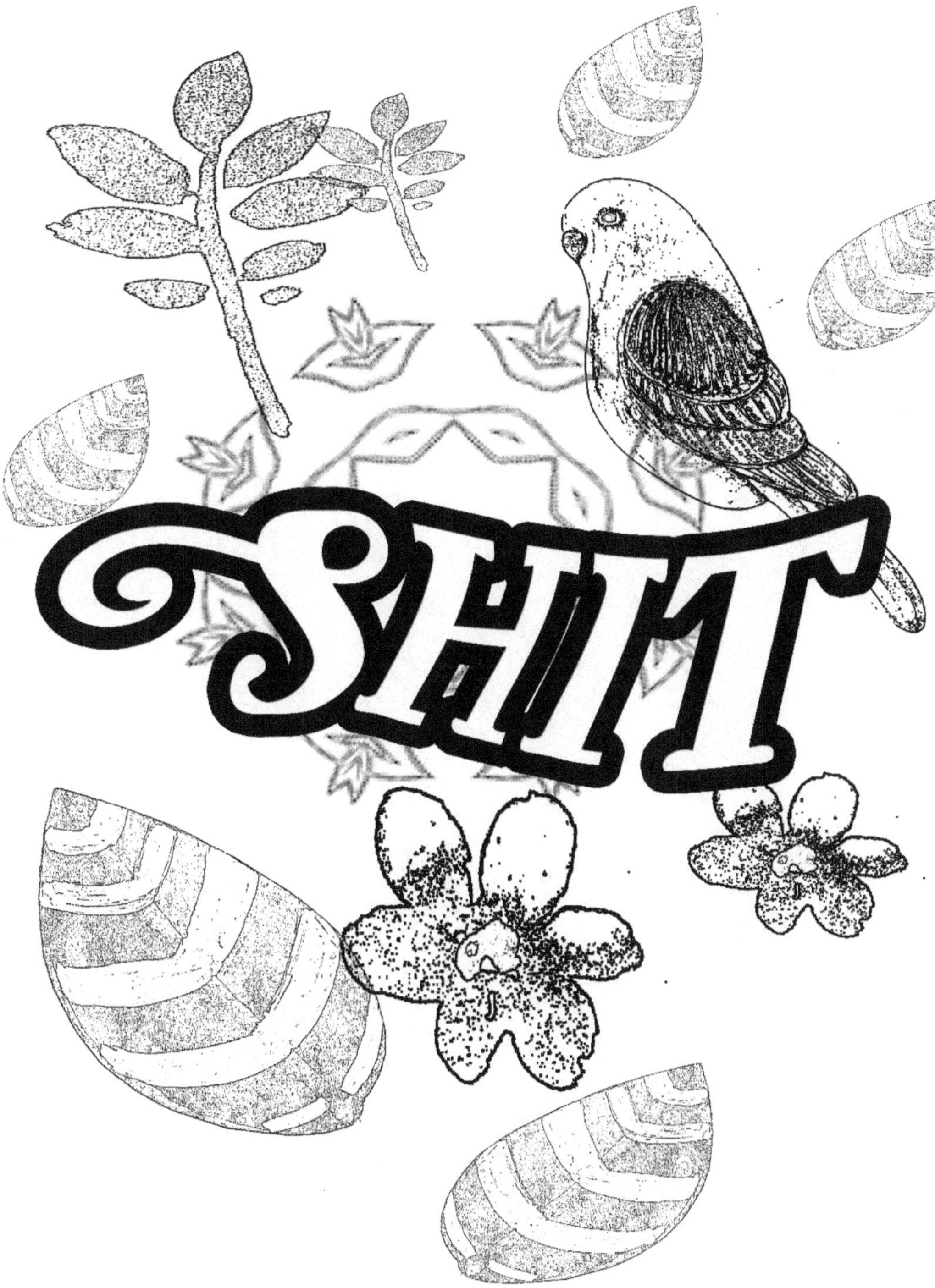
SHIT

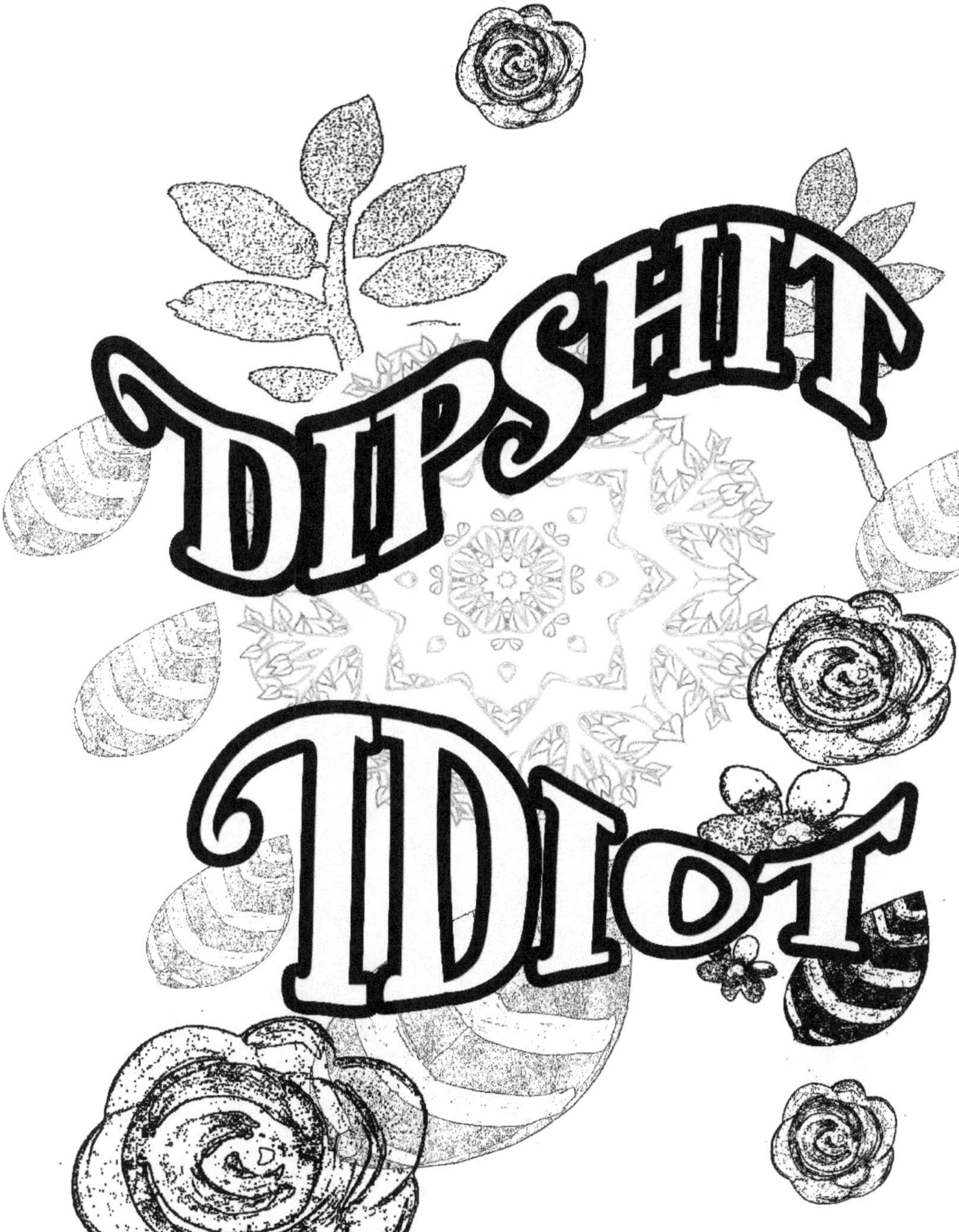
DIPSHIT
IDIOT

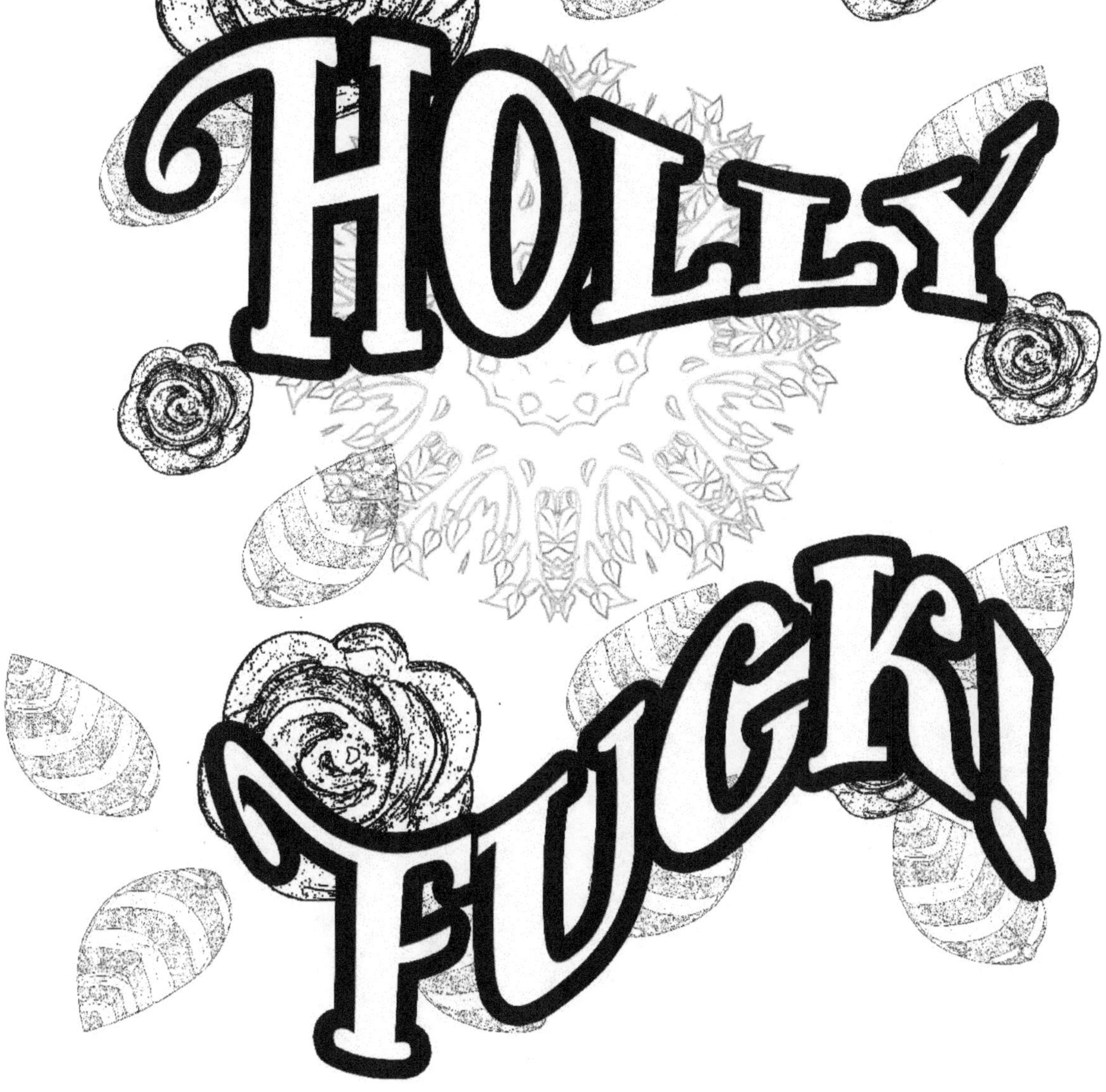
HOLLY
FUCK!

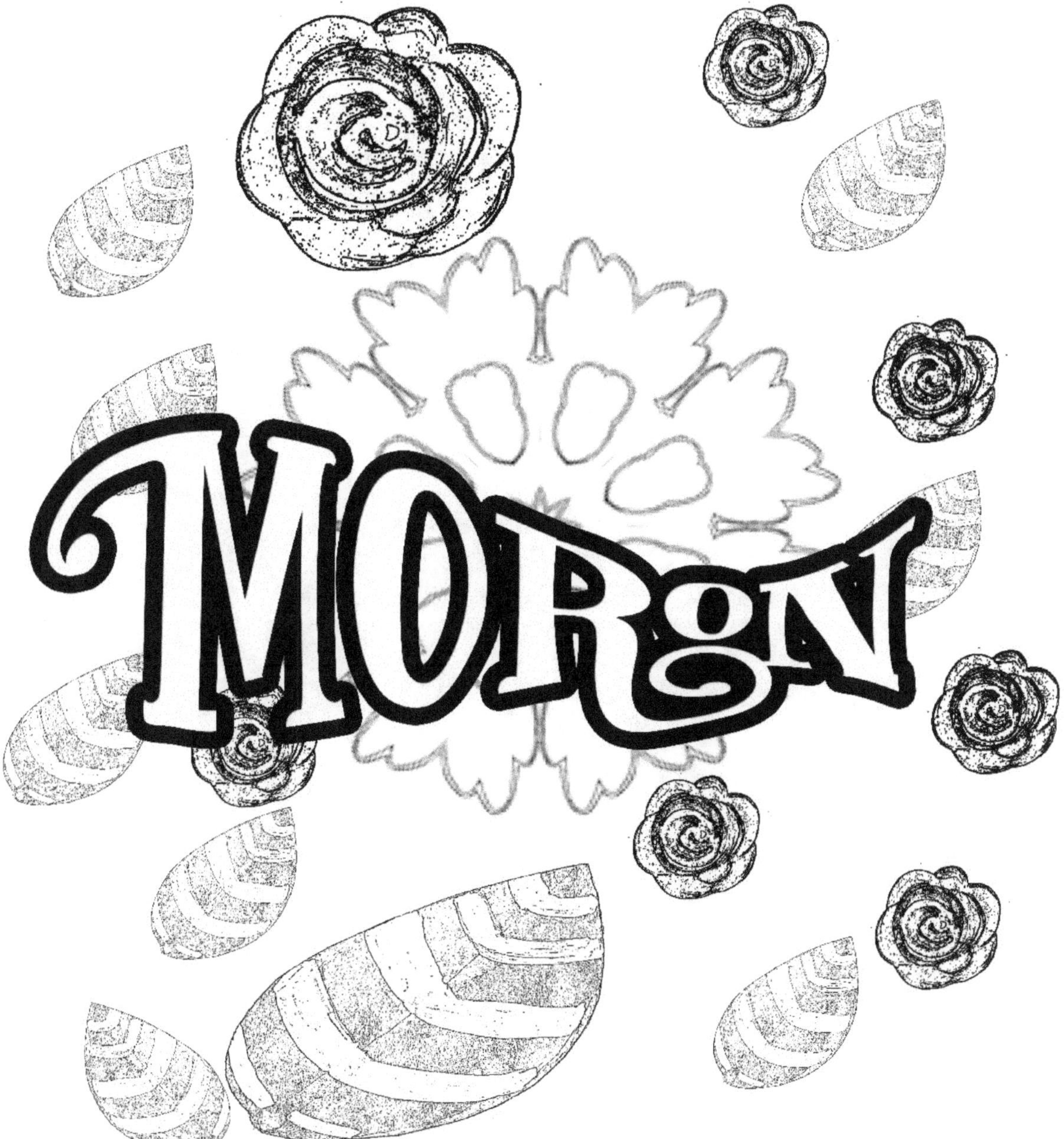
MORON

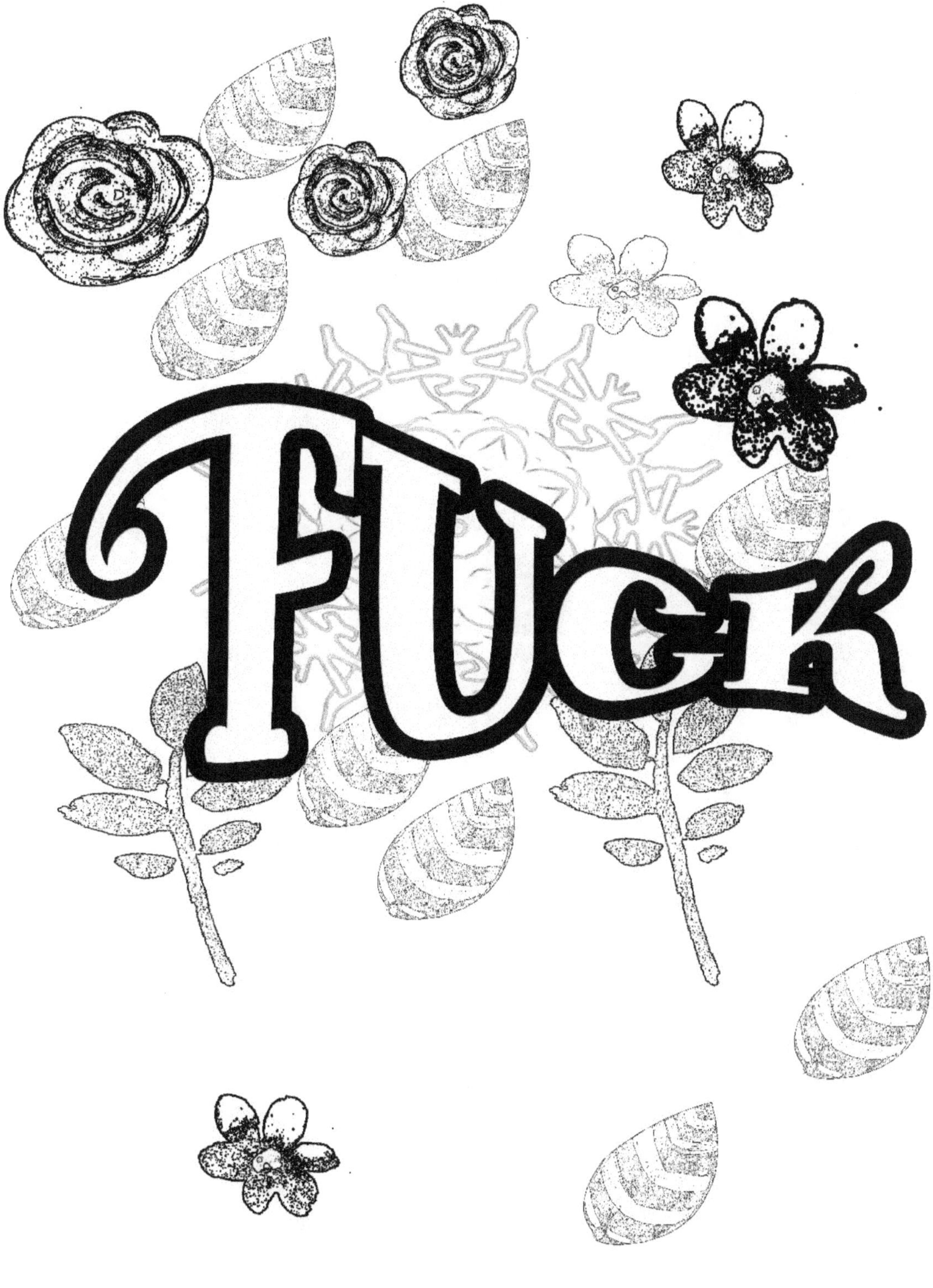
Fuck

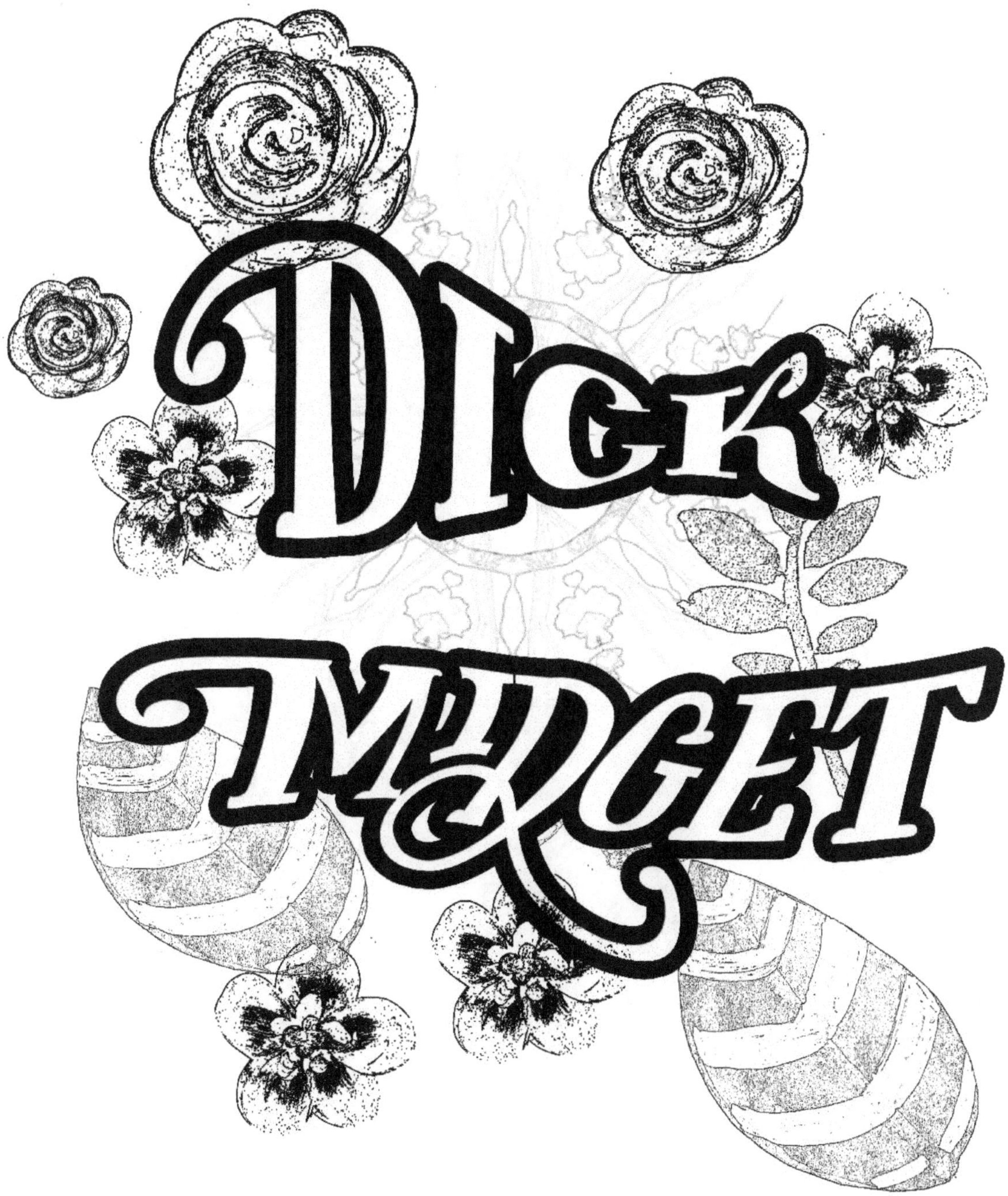
DICK
MIDGET

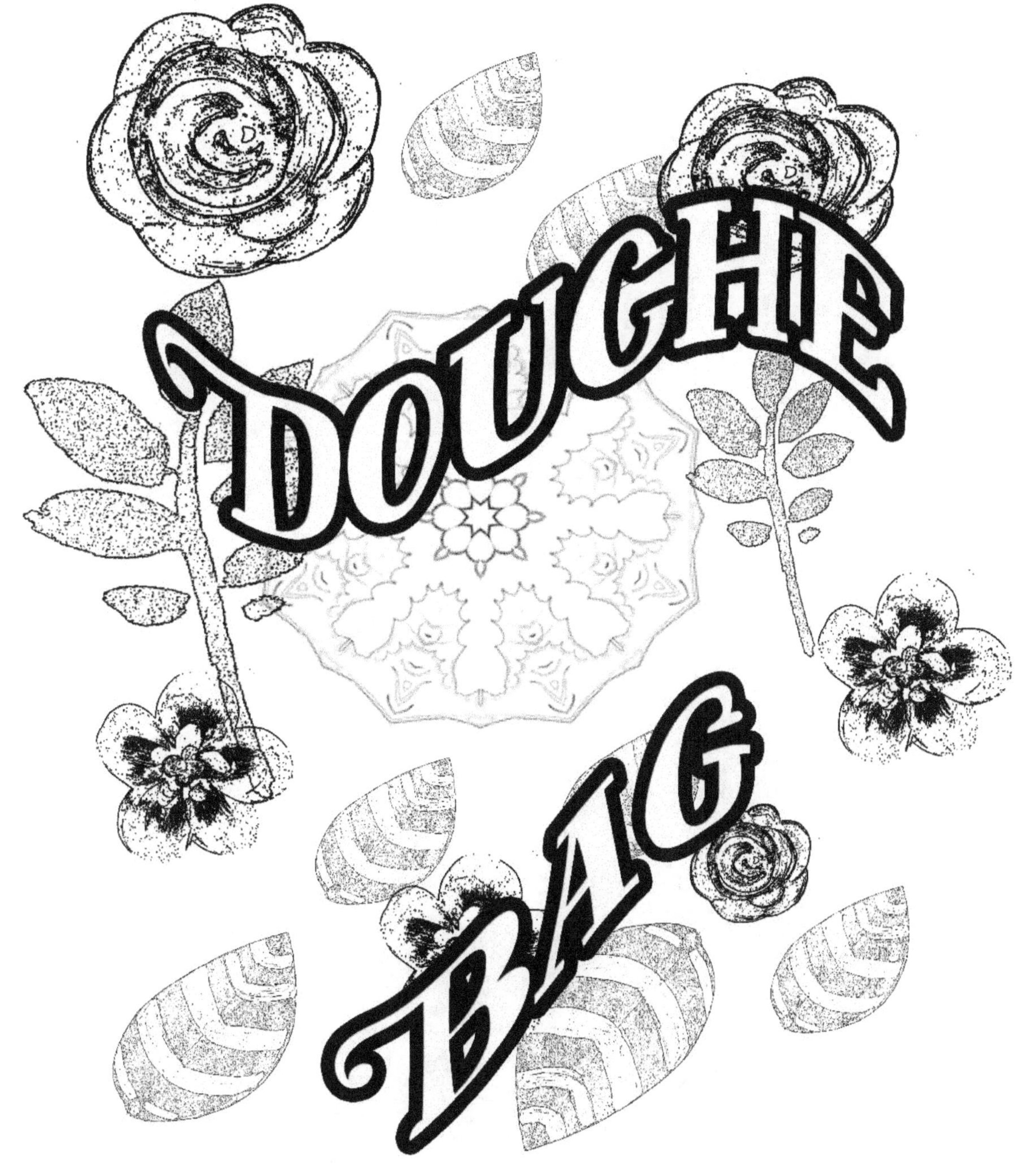
DOUCHE
BAG

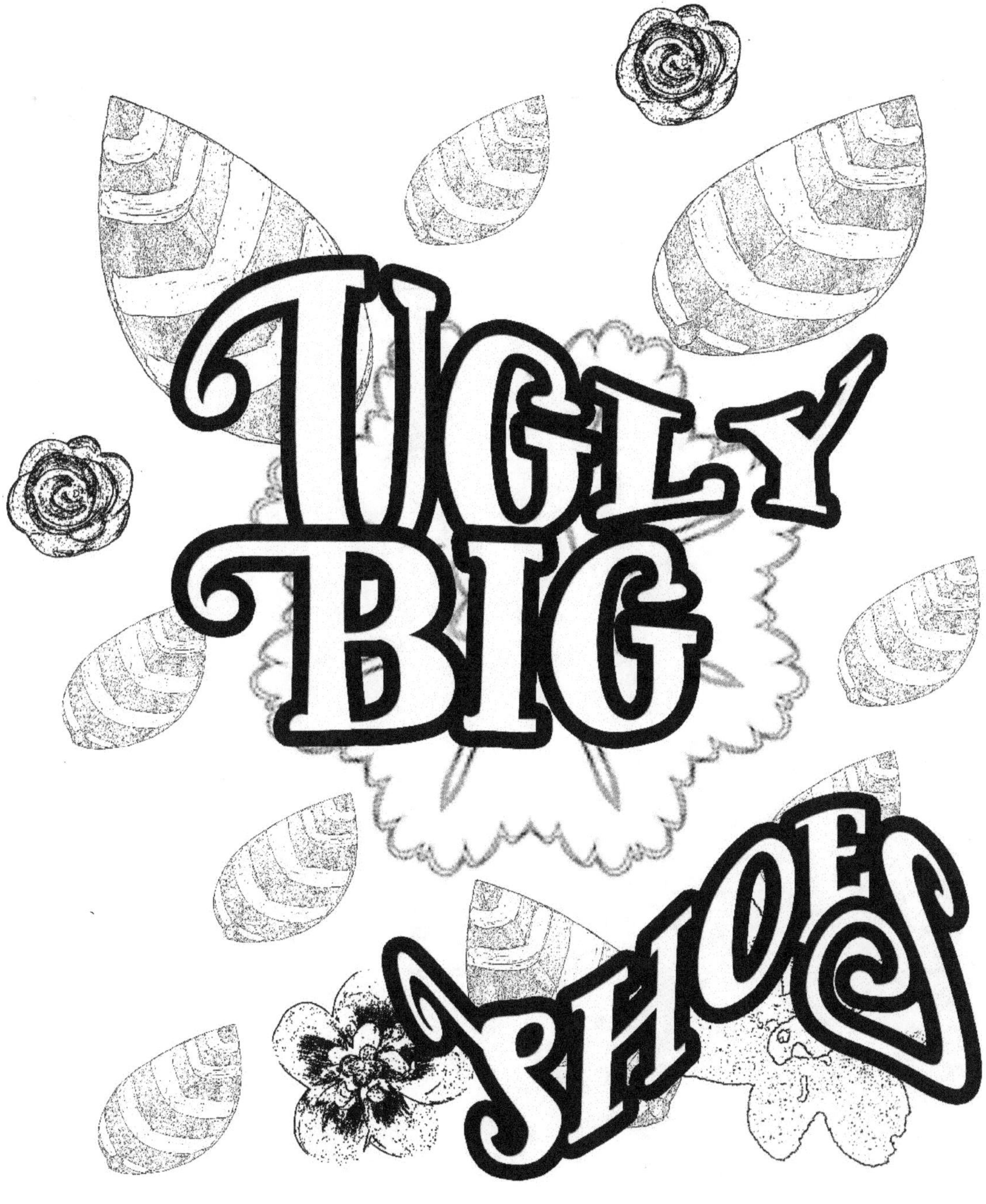
UGLY
BIG
SHOES

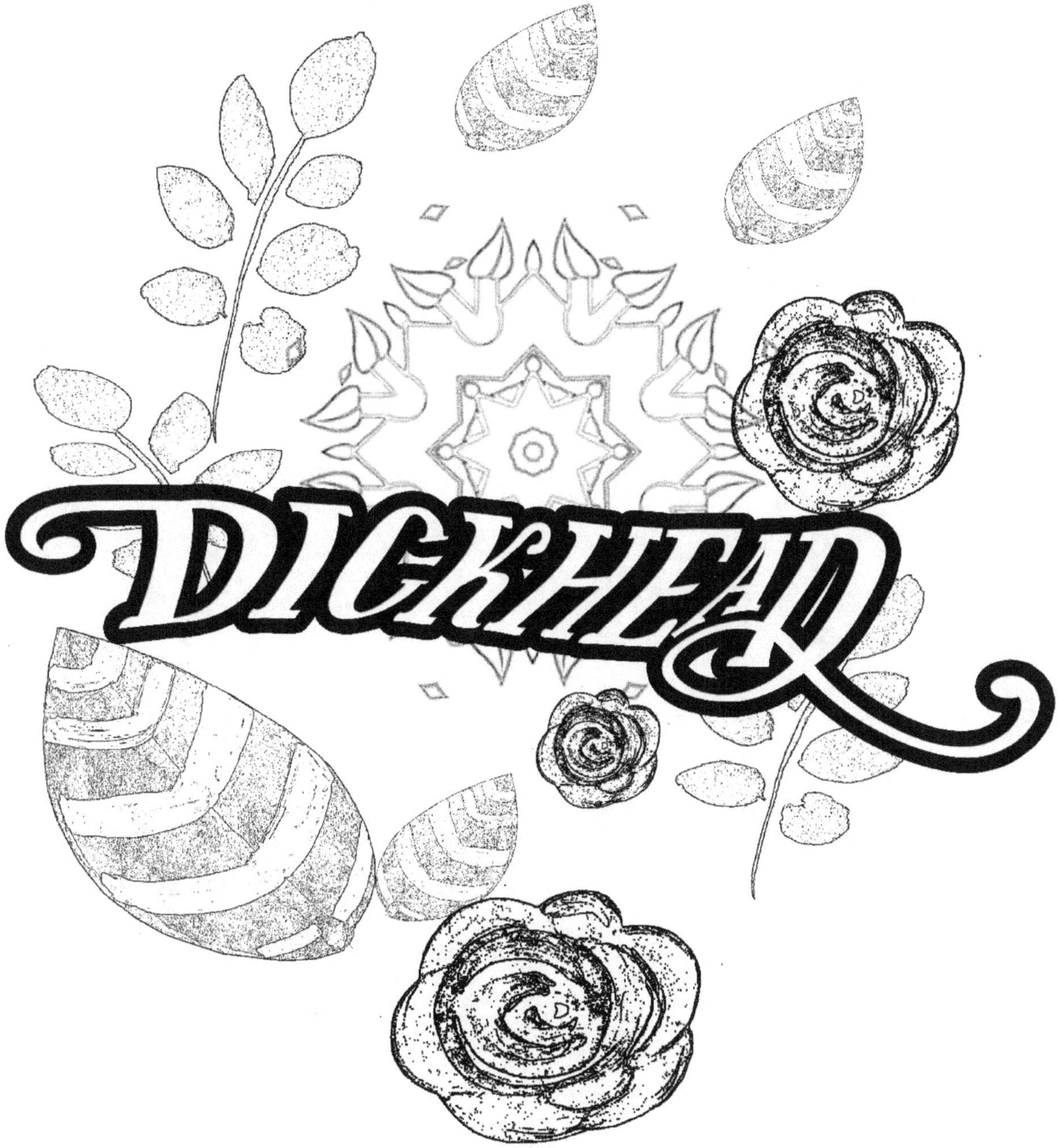
DICKHEAD

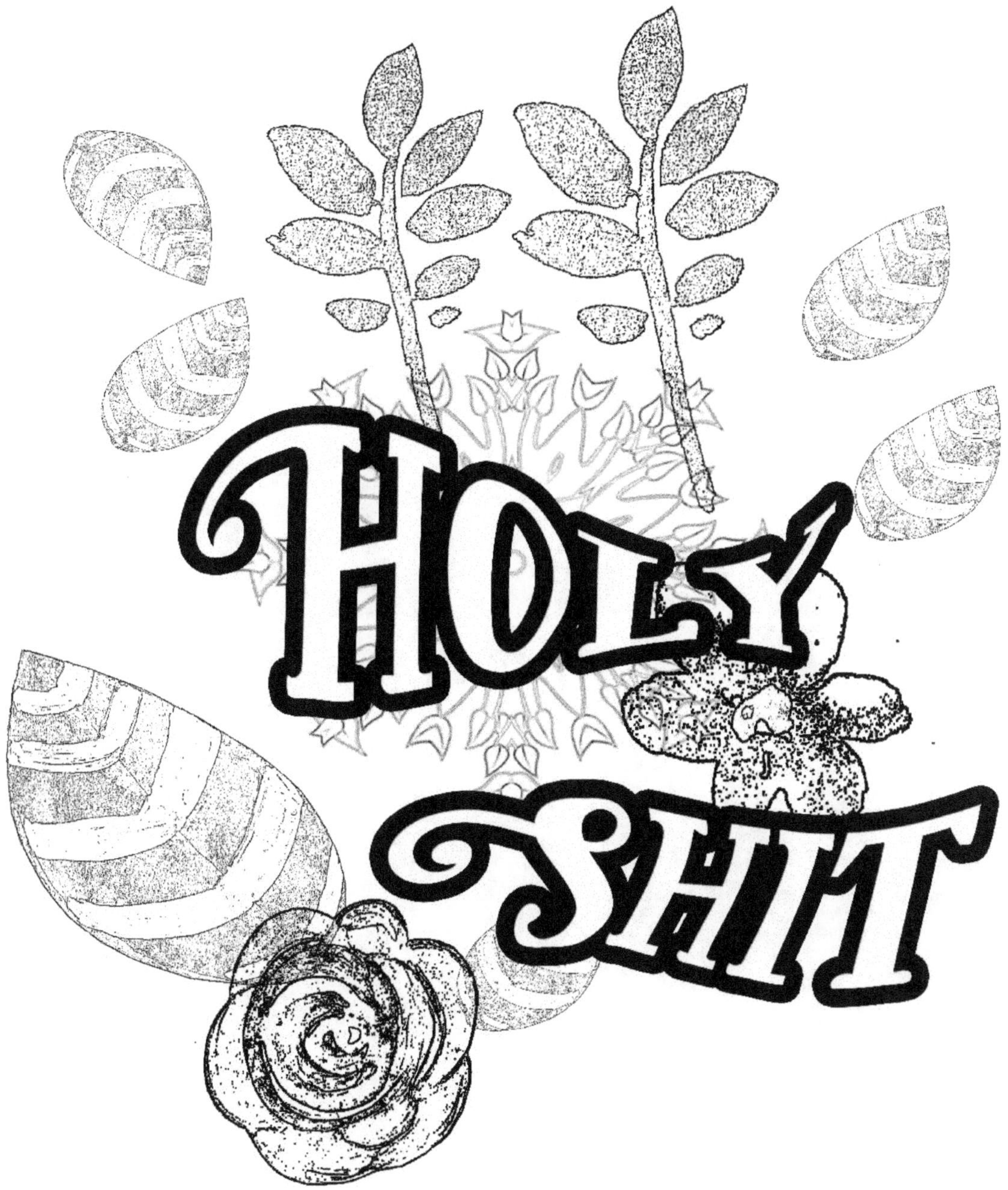
HOLY
SHIT

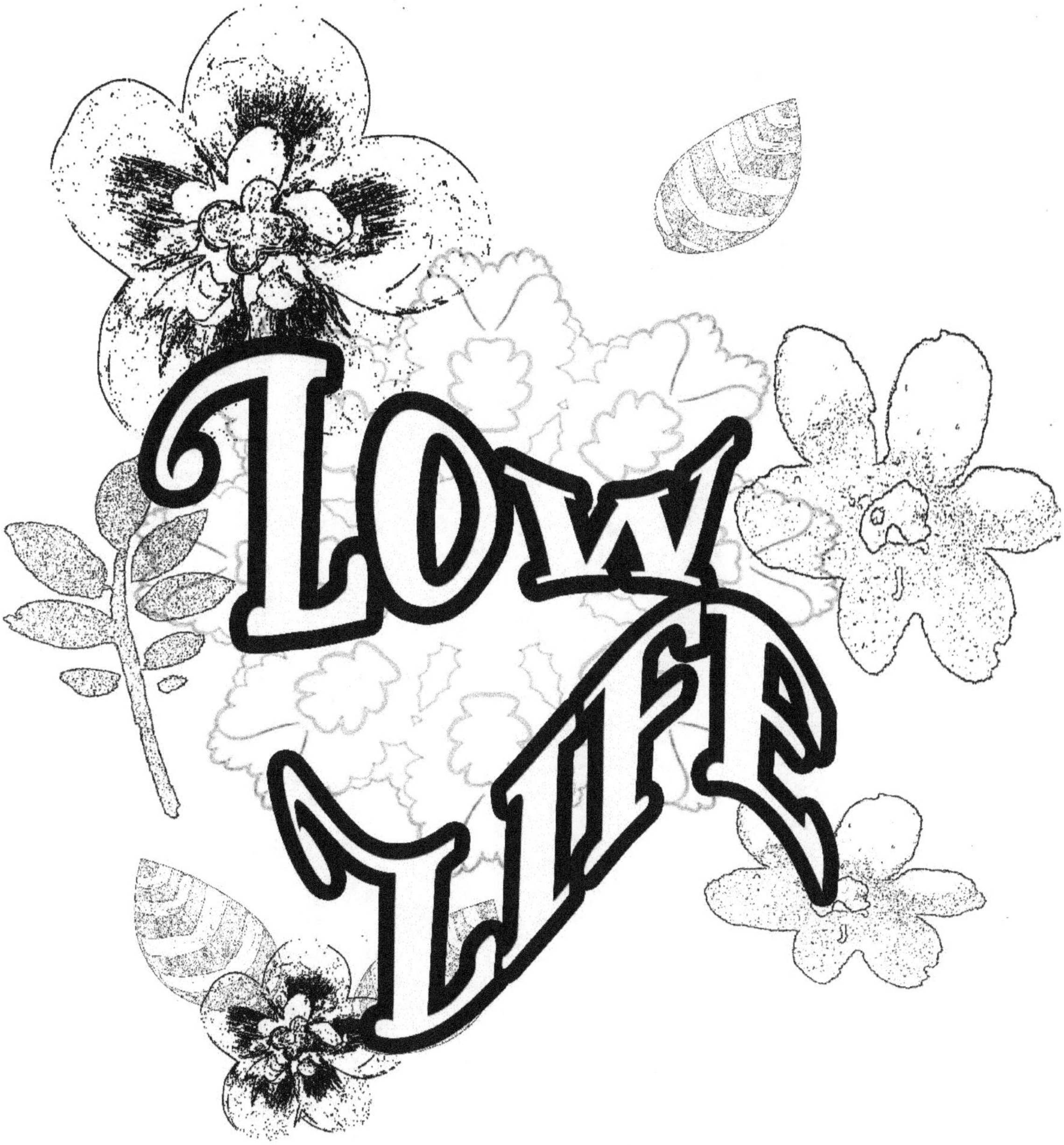
Low
Life

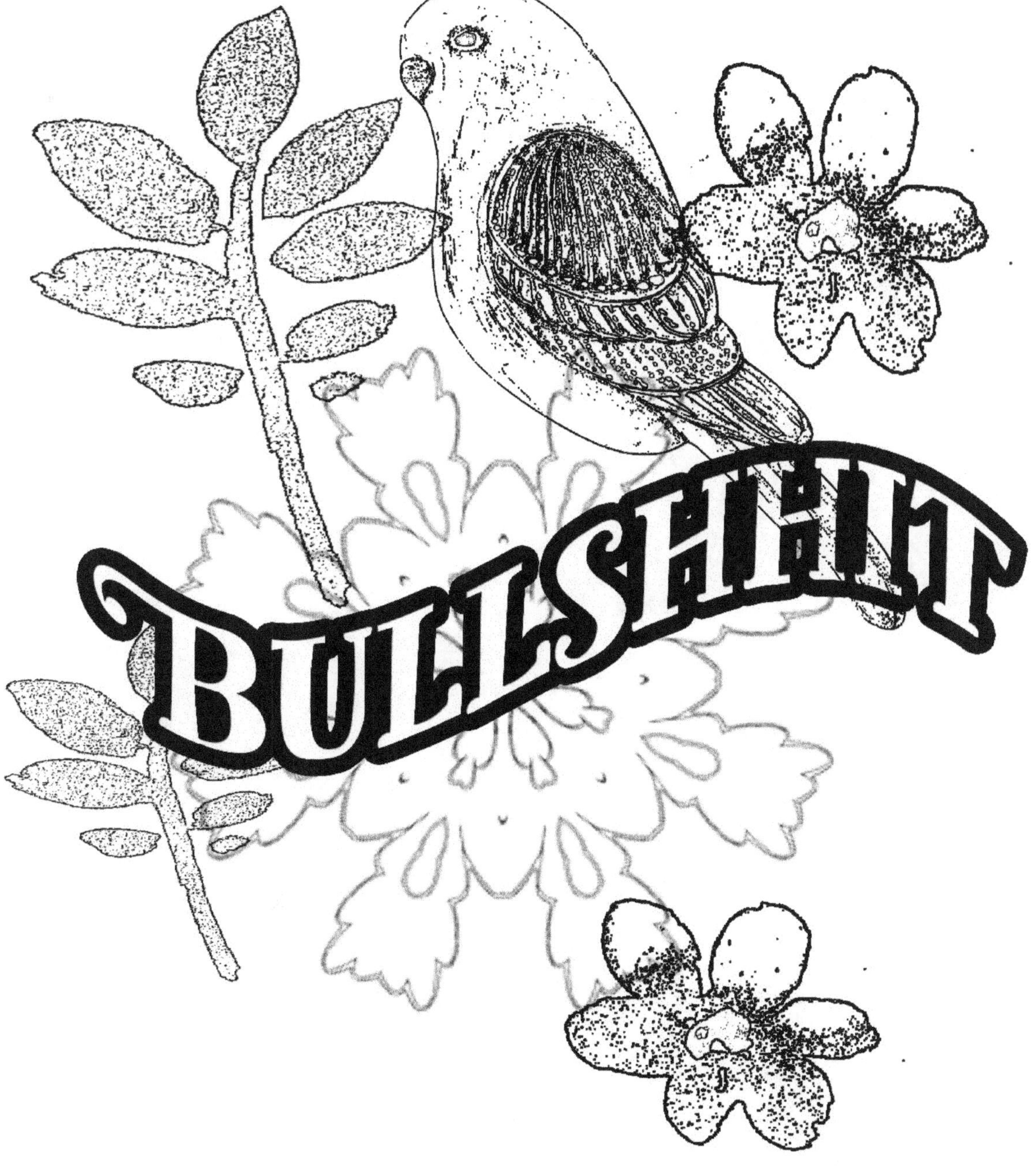
BULLSHIT

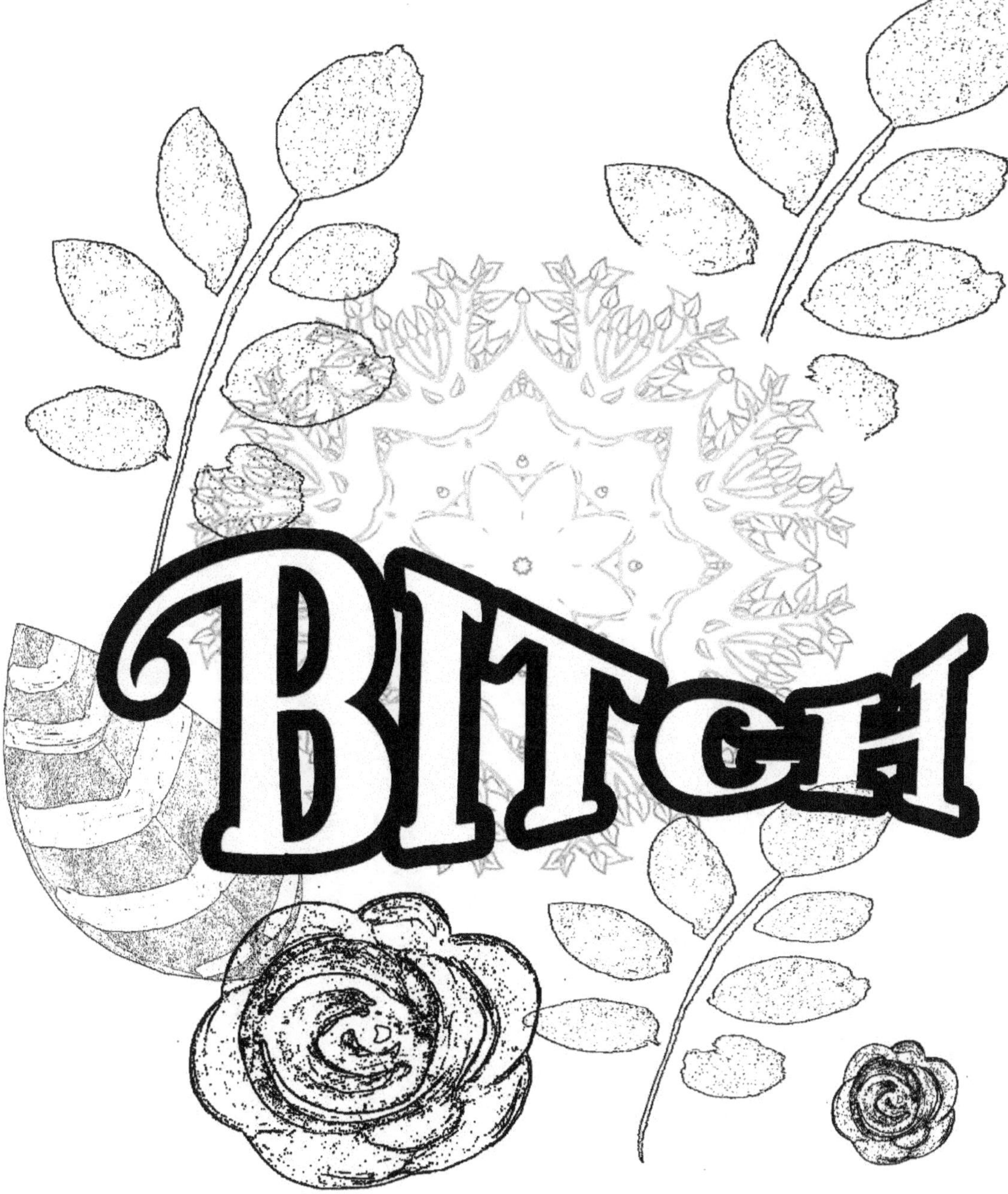
BITCH

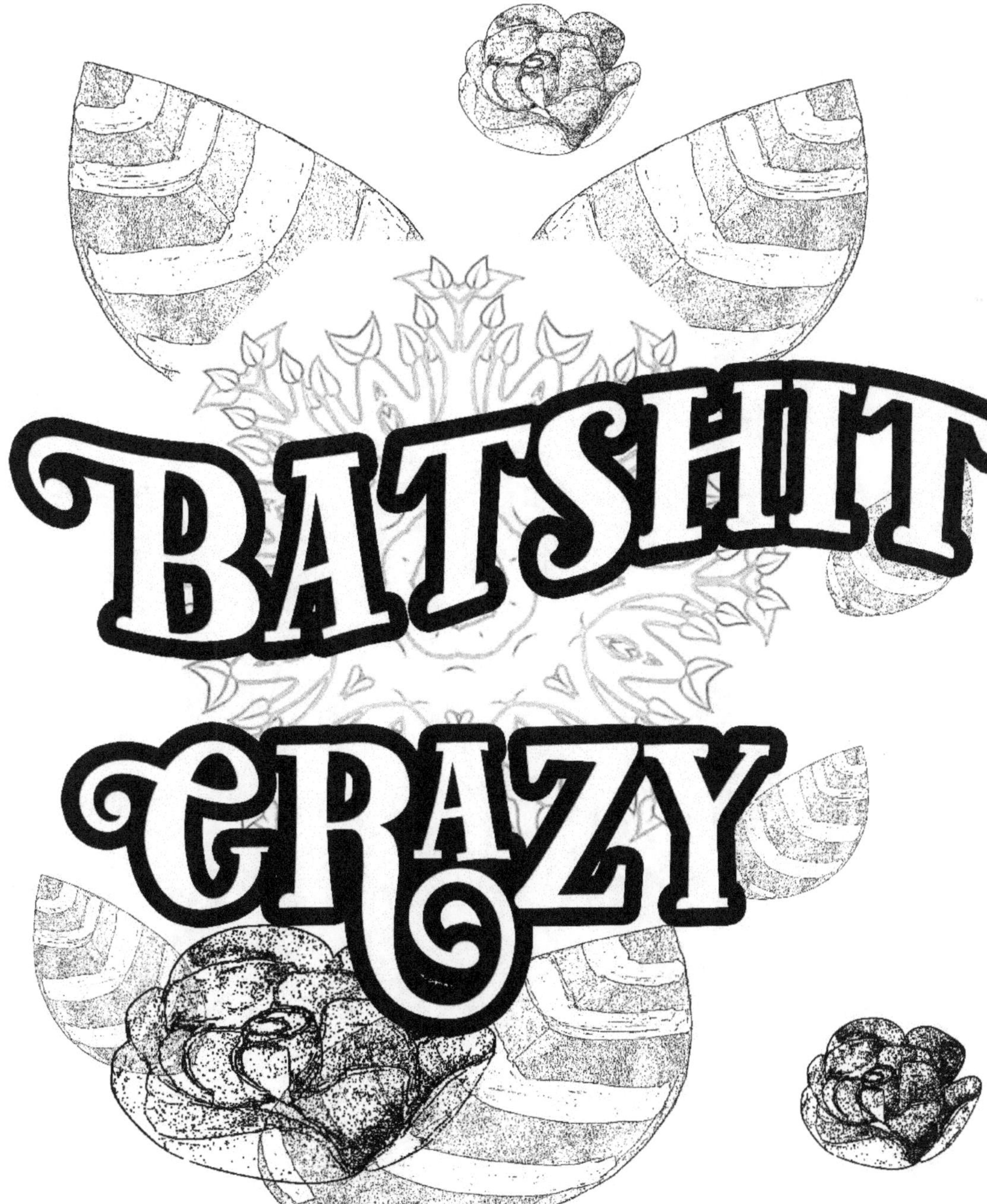
BATSHIT
CRAZY

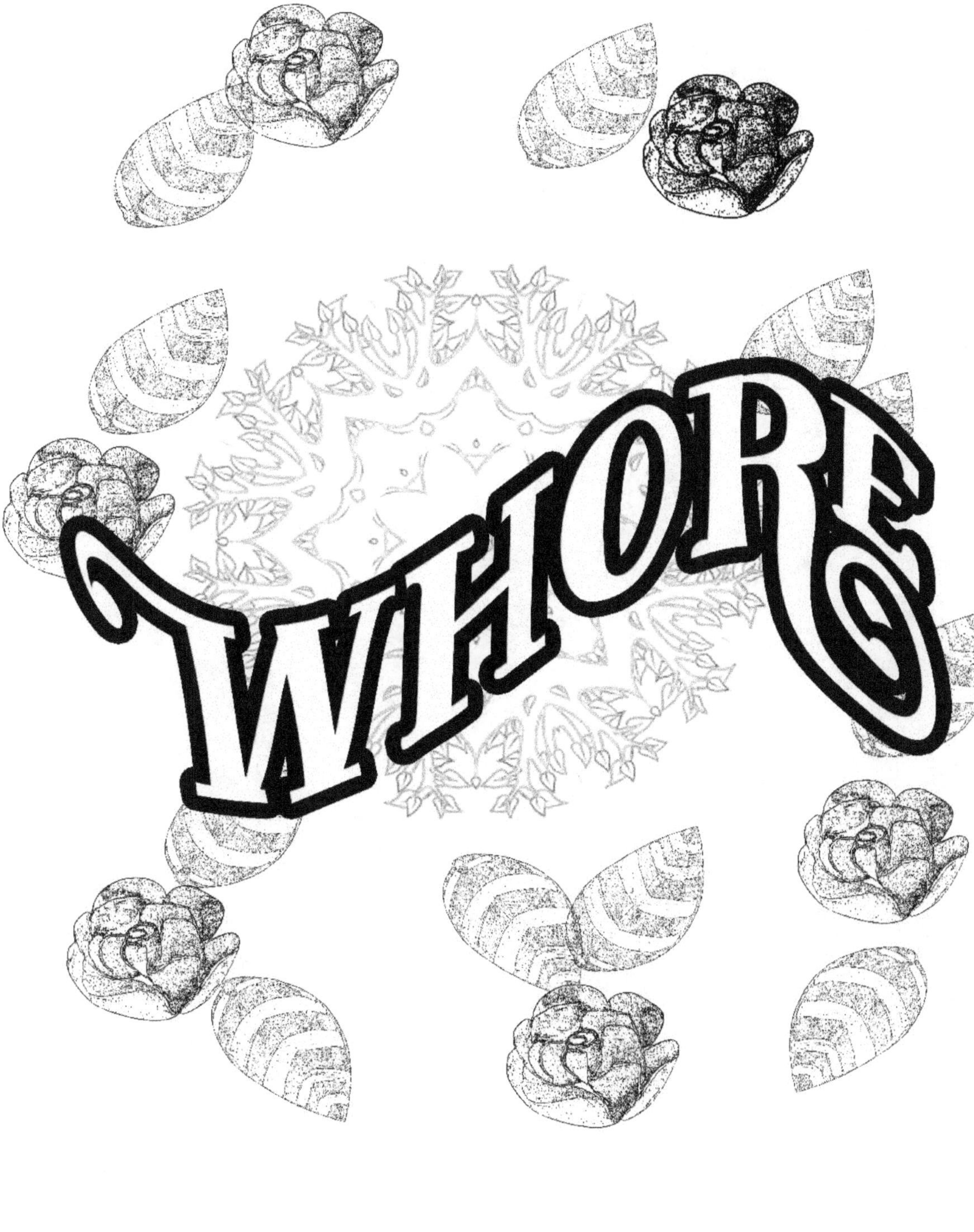
WHORE

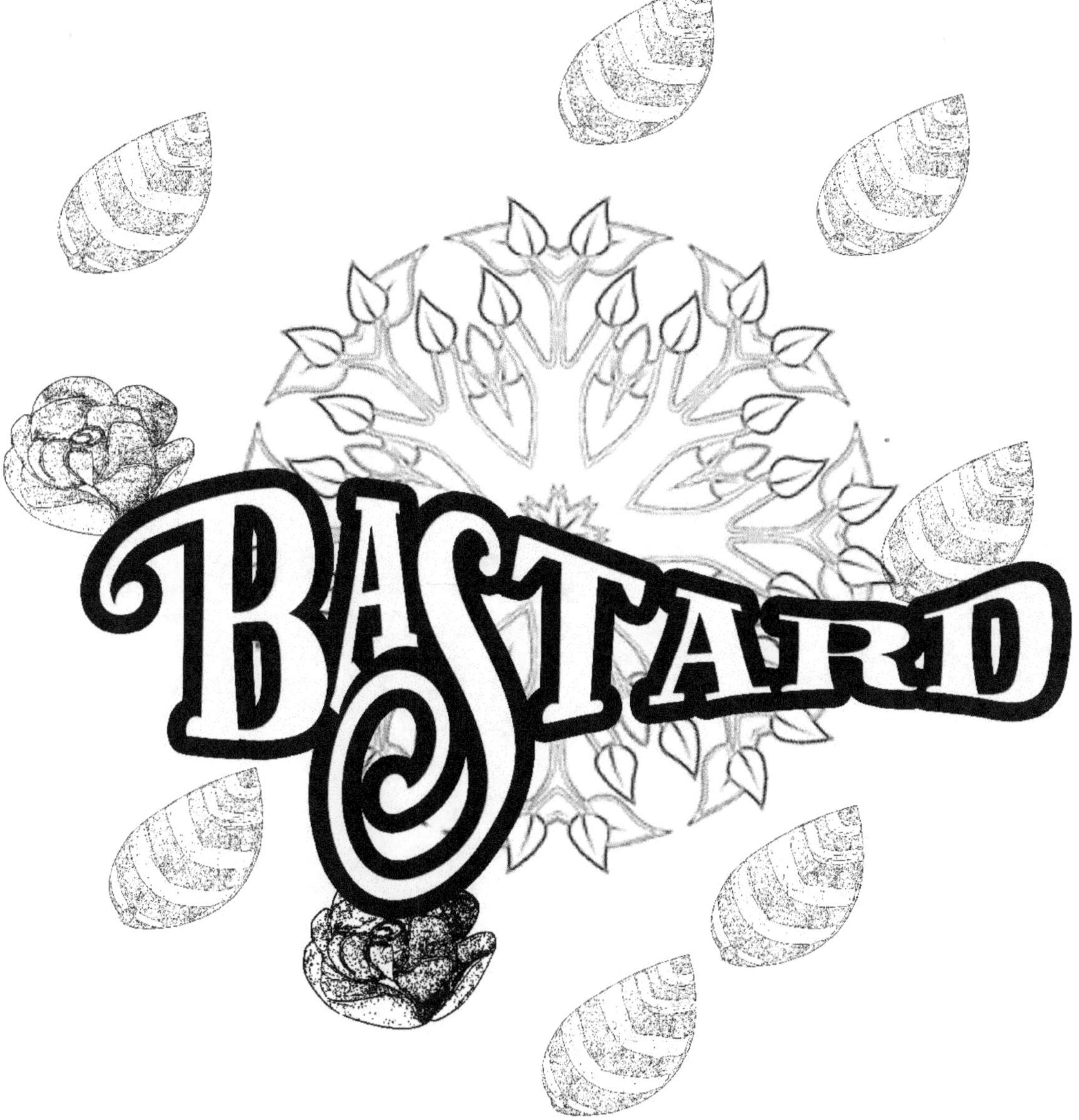
BASTARD

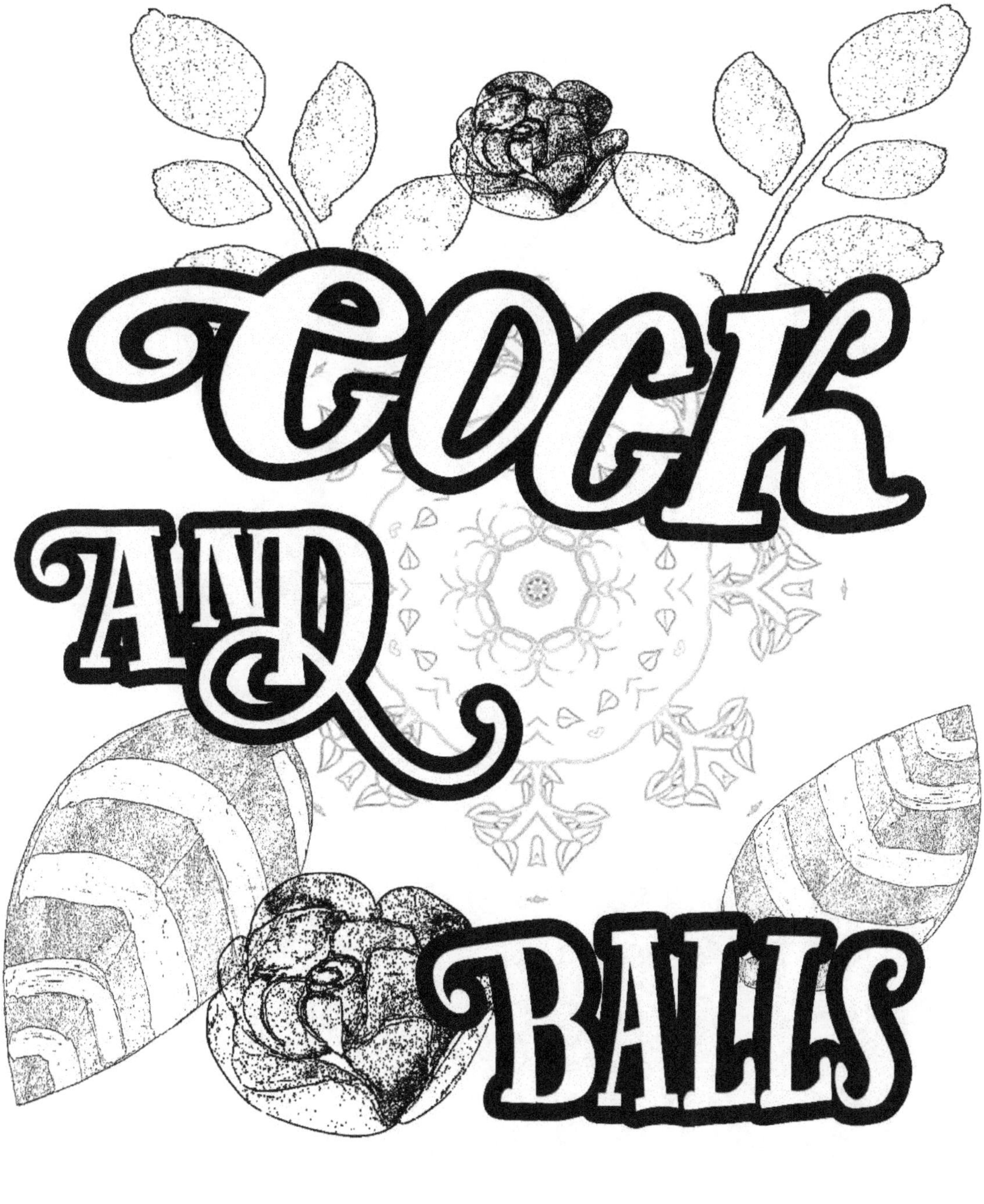
COCK
AND
BALLS

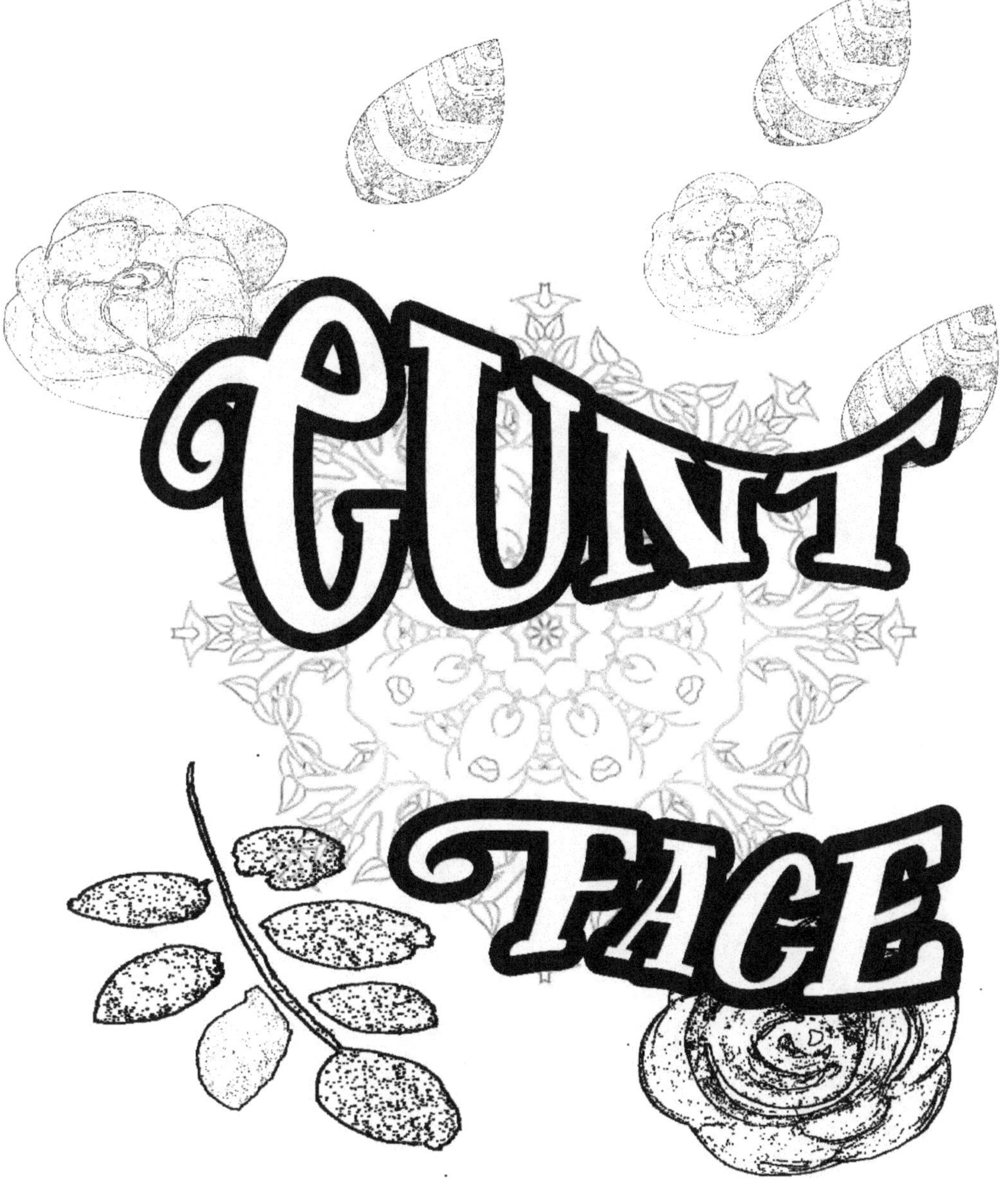
CUNT
FACE

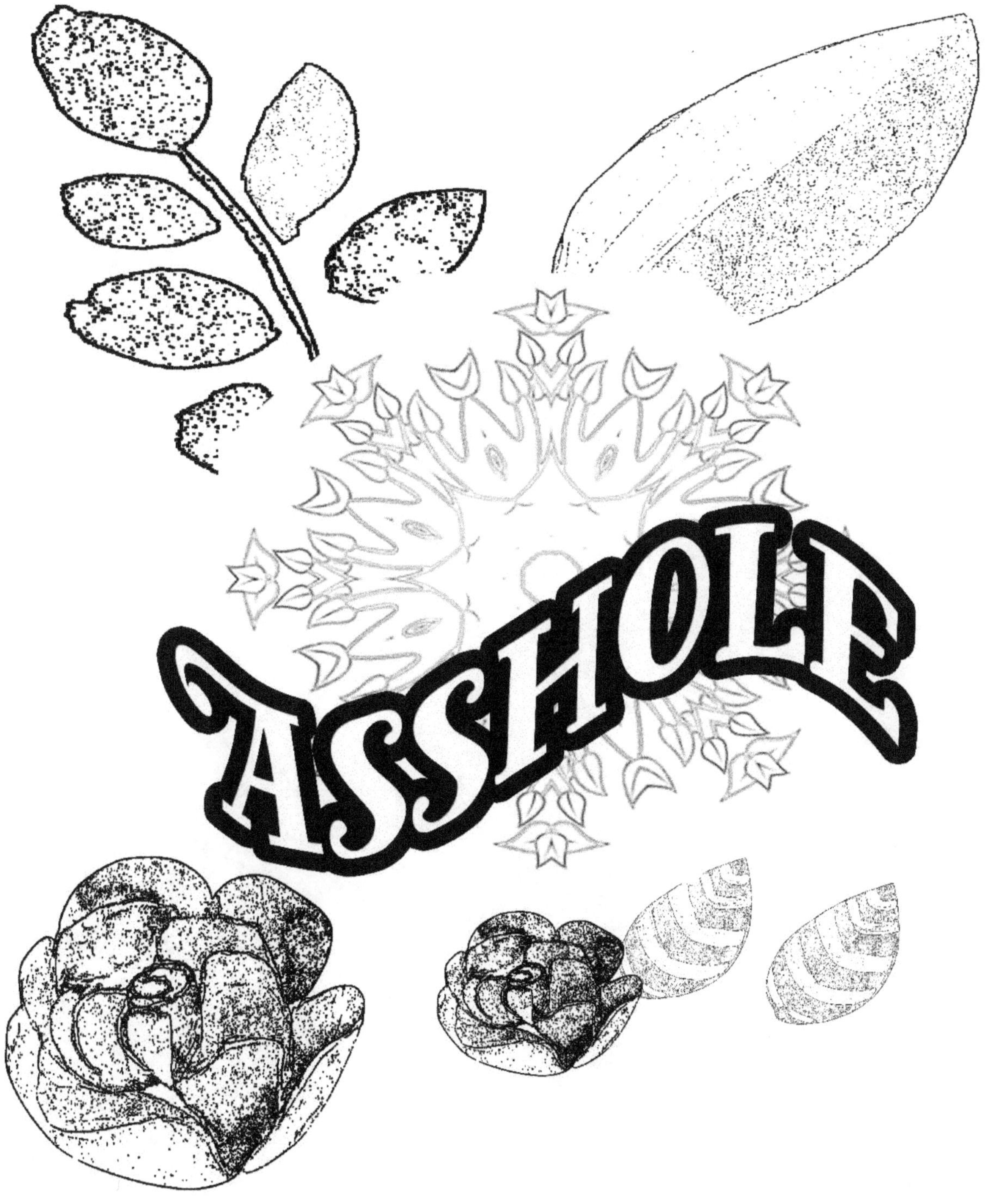
ASSHOLE

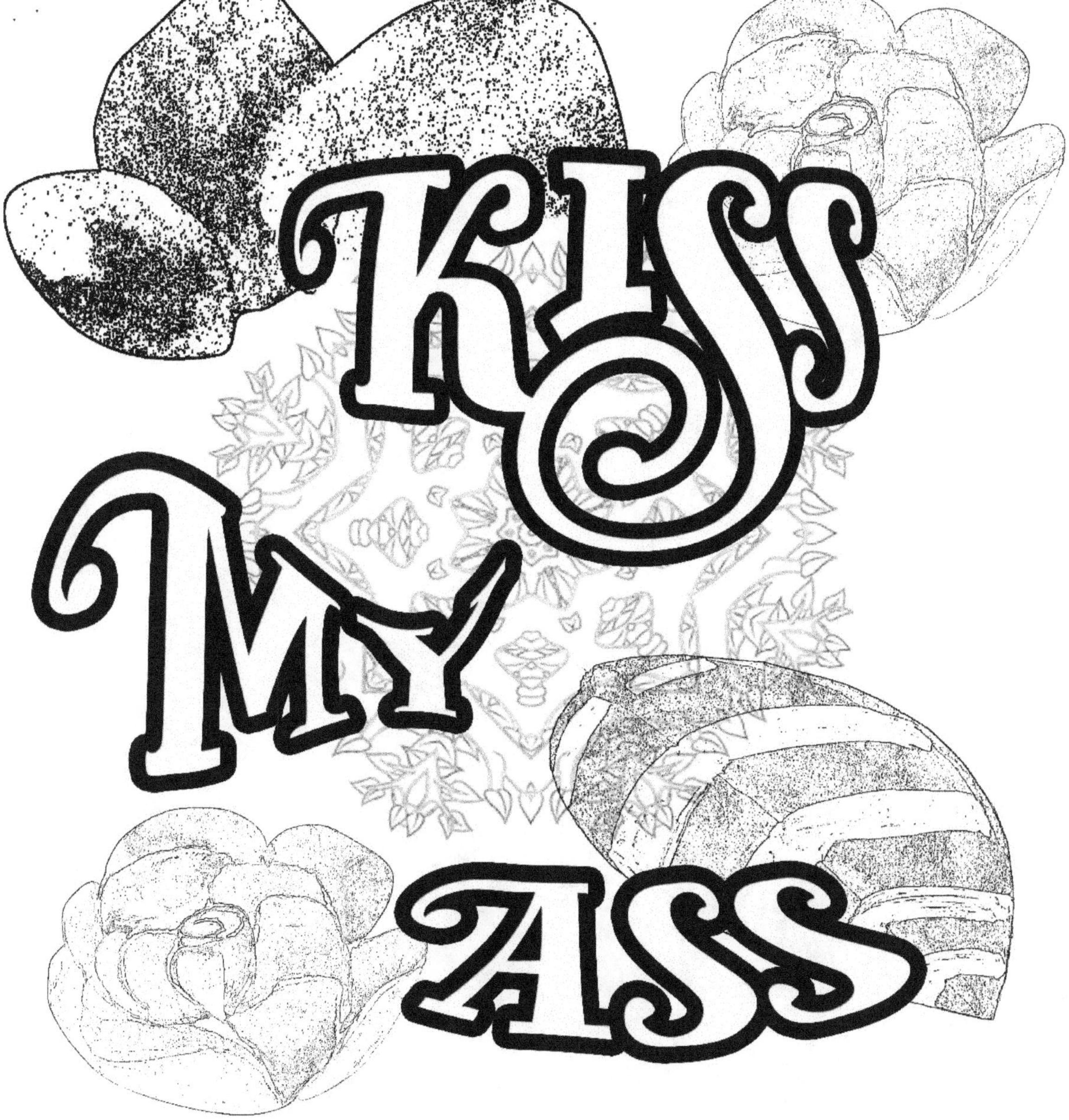
KISS
MY
ASS

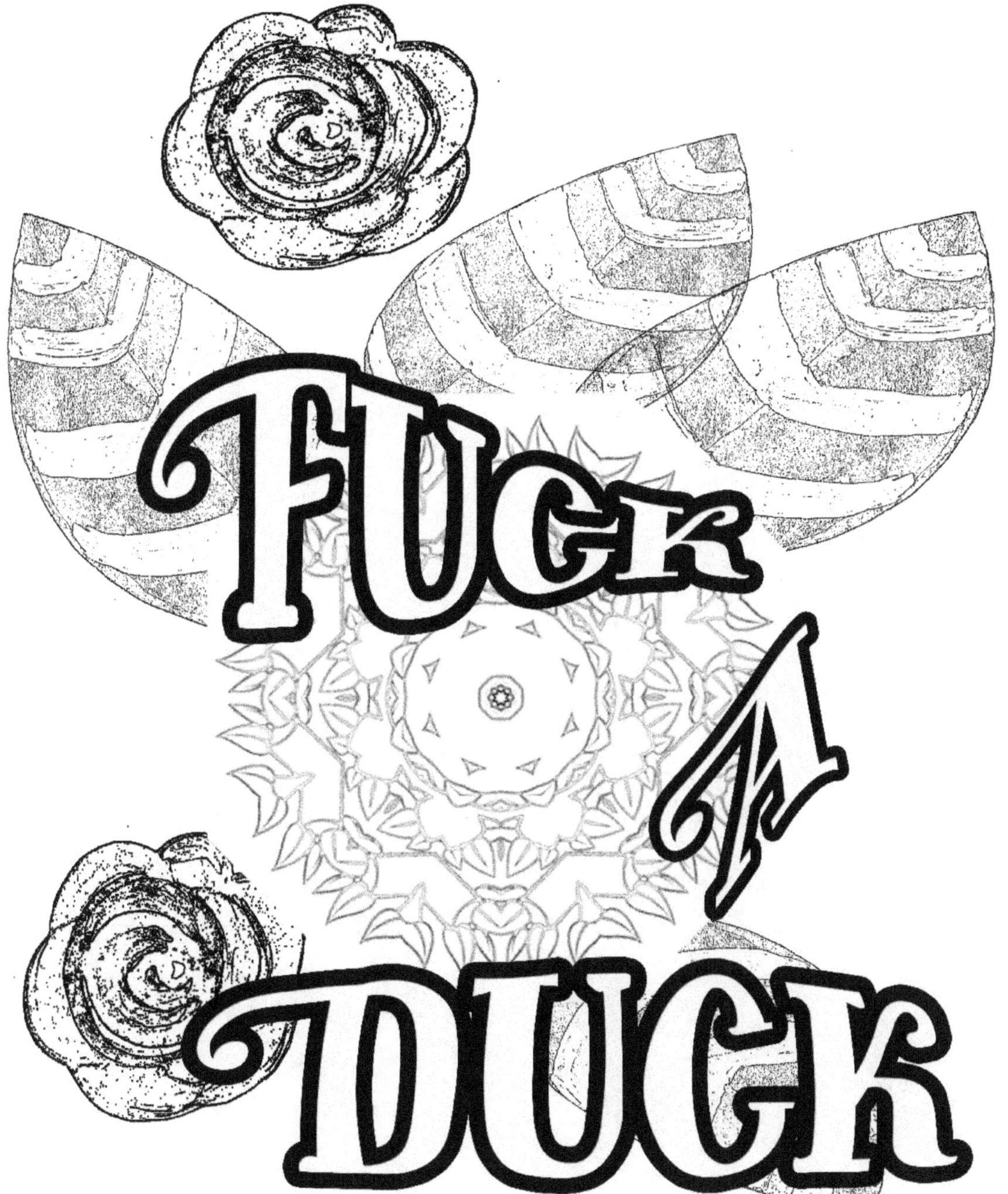
FUCK
A
DUCK

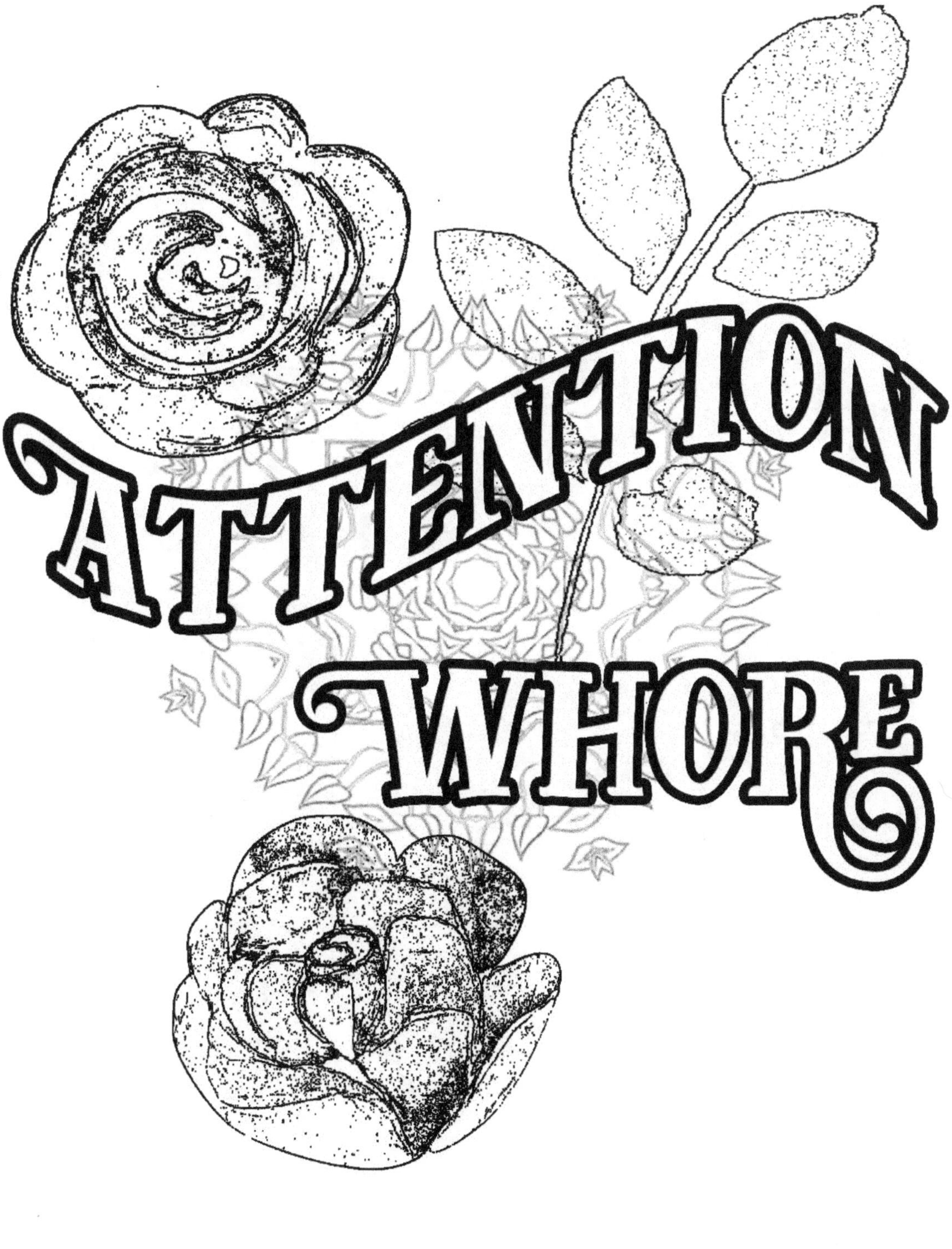
ATTENTION
WHORE

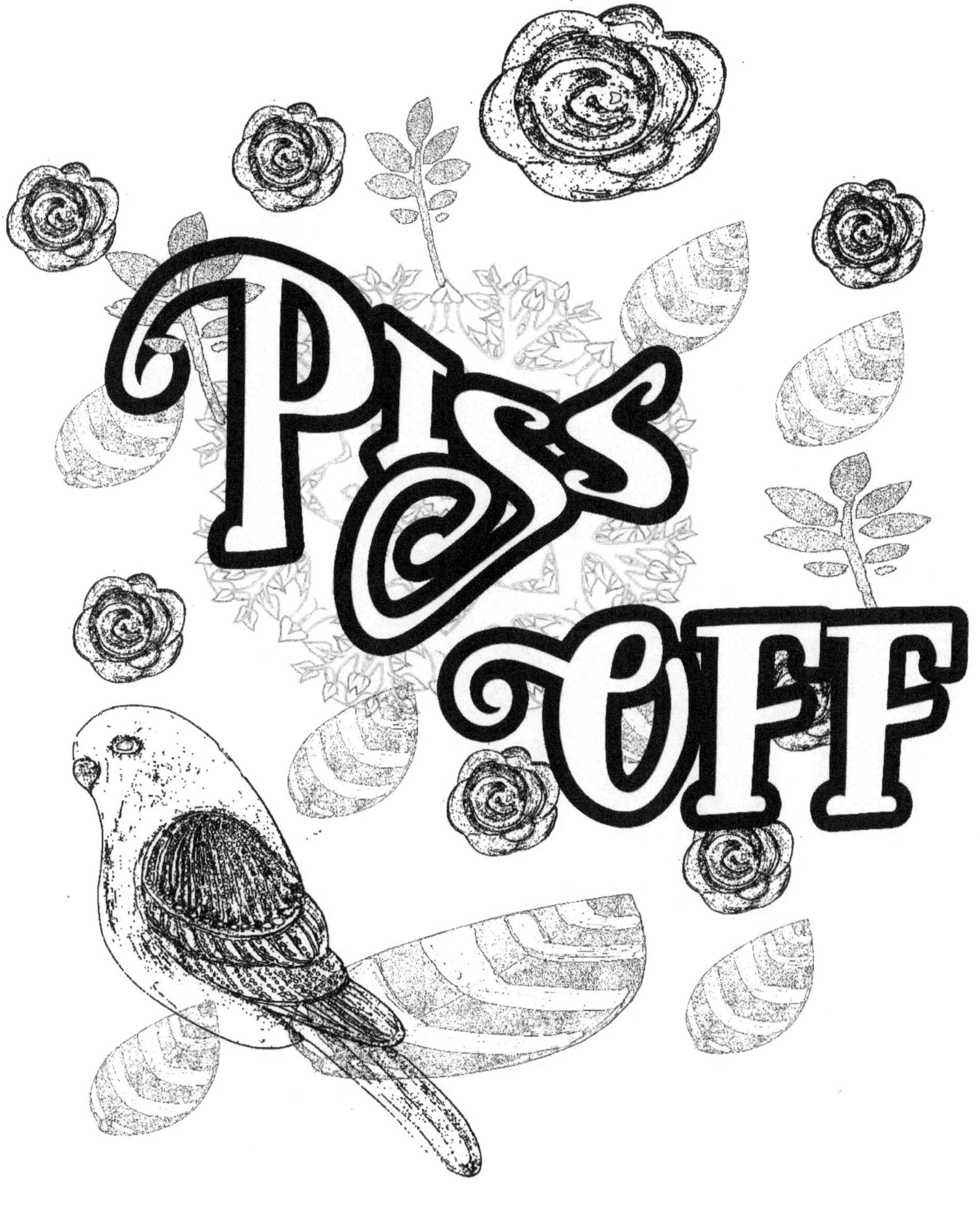
Piss off

Note